Vintage Holiday Coloring Pages: A Nostalgic Christmas Coloring Book for Adults with Classic Christmas Scenes of Antique times

Relax and Unwind with Old World Christmas Designs and Classic Holiday Art for a Timeless Coloring Experience

Beatrice Winter

"This book is a tribute to the cherished traditions that make the holidays magical. Whether you're reconnecting with memories of Christmas past or creating new ones with each stroke of color, my hope is that this book brings you the same sense of joy and wonder that inspired its creation. From my family to yours, wishing you a season filled with beauty, warmth, and love."
- Beatrice Winter

Foreword

"Christmas is not a time nor a season, but a state of mind. To cherish peace and goodwill, to be plenteous in mercy, is to have the real spirit of Christmas." — Calvin Coolidge

Welcome to An Old-Fashioned Christmas: A Coloring Book for Adults, a heartfelt journey back in time to the cozy, joyful, and enchanting Christmases of yesteryear. Here, we invite you to step into a world filled with nostalgic charm, where twinkling lights, rustic ornaments, snow-covered cottages, and timeless holiday traditions come to life through the stroke of your colored pencils.

This book draws from cherished traditions of Christmases past, inspired by the elegance of Victorian holiday decor, the rustic charm of rural festivities, and the timeless warmth of family celebrations. Each design reflects elements of bygone eras—whether it's the intricate patterns of antique ornaments, the romantic coziness of horse-drawn sleighs, or the quaint serenity of a snow-covered village. By bringing these historical elements to life on paper, this book offers not just a creative outlet, but a nostalgic journey through holiday traditions that shaped the way we celebrate today.

Coloring isn't just a pastime for children; it's a rejuvenating and creative escape for adults too, with benefits that extend far beyond the paper and ink. Recent research has revealed just how powerful this seemingly simple activity can be for our overall well-being. In a study conducted by the University of the West of England, researchers found that 73% of participants experienced a significant reduction in anxiety and stress levels after just 20 minutes of focused coloring. This effect isn't surprising when you consider the science: engaging in structured coloring has been shown to activate the parts of the brain associated with mindfulness and relaxation.

But the perks don't end with stress relief. Coloring also taps into our natural creativity, boosting mood and providing an effective way to practice self-care. Dr. Stan Rodski, a neuroscientist who has explored the effects of coloring on the brain, explains that the repetitive motions and focused attention involved in coloring can produce a meditative state, lowering the heart rate and activating the amygdala to produce feelings of calm. In fact, a study published in Art Therapy: Journal of the American Art Therapy Association found that individuals who participated in coloring experienced a 60% increase in mental clarity and focus.

"It is Christmas in the heart that puts Christmas in the air." — W.T. Ellis

So, why an old-fashioned Christmas?
In today's fast-paced, technology-driven world, it's easy to get caught up in the busyness of everyday life, especially during the holiday season. There's something uniquely comforting about revisiting the simpler, more meaningful celebrations of days gone by. An old-fashioned Christmas brings to mind the warmth of family gatherings, the smell of fresh pine and homemade cookies, the glow of candlelit windows, and the joyous carols sung by loved ones huddled together in the snow. It was a time when the holiday spirit wasn't measured by lavish gifts or digital displays but by the heartfelt traditions passed down from generation to generation.

An Old-Fashioned Christmas invites you to slow down, unwind, and savor these simple yet profound pleasures. As you immerse yourself in these intricate designs and festive scenes, you'll be transported to a world where the holiday spirit feels authentic and unhurried. This nostalgic theme not only brings a sense of warmth and coziness but also reminds us of the timeless values of connection, gratitude, and joy. From classic Victorian carolers to serene winter landscapes, each illustration has been carefully crafted to evoke a warm sense of nostalgia and wonder.

To make the most of your coloring journey, consider these simple tips:

- **Create Your Perfect Setting:** Set up your coloring space with soft lighting, a festive playlist, or the warm scent of cinnamon candles to immerse yourself in the holiday spirit.
- **Experiment with Mediums:** While colored pencils are a classic choice, don't hesitate to try other mediums like gel pens, watercolor pencils, or fine-tip markers for added vibrancy and texture.

- **Personalize Your Palette:** Don't feel limited by traditional colors—let your imagination guide you. Perhaps the carolers' scarves glow in pastel hues, or the snow sparkles with a touch of gold or silver.
- **Add Your Own Details:** Bring extra life to the designs by adding personal touches, such as tiny snowflakes, patterns on clothing, or even hidden messages for loved ones.

So, gather your favorite colored pencils, pour yourself a cup of hot cocoa, and let this coloring book be your sanctuary of peace, joy, and creativity. Whether you're unwinding by the fireplace or simply taking a moment for yourself in the middle of a busy day, know that each colored page is a step toward a more balanced and mindful holiday season. Here's to reliving the splendor of old-fashioned Christmases, one beautiful stroke at a time.

Book Reviews

"The scenes in this book are so evocative and full of charm. I love how the pages remind me of stories I heard growing up, and I feel like a kid again every time I color. It's the perfect mix of relaxation and holiday cheer!"
— Victoria Grant, Rochester, NY

"I bought this book as a way to practice mindfulness, and it has truly brought me so much joy. The old-fashioned Christmas theme is just lovely, and each page tells a story I'm happy to bring to life with color. It's a wonderful way to slow down and soak in the spirit of the season."
— David Reynolds, Boulder, CO

"This book is a holiday tradition in itself! Coloring these pages takes me back to simpler times and fills me with Christmas spirit. My friends and I even hosted a coloring night, and we all agreed it was a magical experience. Highly recommended!"
— Samantha Lin, Chicago, IL

"A beautiful blend of art and nostalgia. I never realized how calming coloring could be until I got this book. It has helped me manage holiday stress, and I've rediscovered the simple joy of Christmas through every illustration."
— Karen Fletcher, Williamsburg, VA

"Before beginning, take a moment to pause and focus on your breath. Allow yourself to fully engage with the process—observe the textures, the colors, and the steady rhythm of your strokes. If your mind begins to wander, gently guide your attention back to the page. This simple practice can enhance the meditative quality of coloring, leaving you feeling more present and grounded."

Whispers Of A Timeless Christmas

A quiet snow falls, crisp and white,
Softly blanketing the world tonight.
Lanterns flicker with golden glow,
While holly wreaths don each window.

A horse-drawn sleigh on cobbled streets,
Echoes of laughter where old friends meet.
Carols sung in frosty air,
Voices lifted in simple prayer.

Candles gleam on piney boughs,
Stockings hung where memories rouse.
Gingerbread scents and cider's steam,
A fire that crackles, a warm-lit dream.

Children giggle and dance with glee,
Eyes wide with wonder at the trimmed-up tree.
And elders tell tales from years gone by,
Of handmade gifts and starlit skies.

It's a season wrapped in tender grace,
A gentle, heartwarming, timeless place.
Where love and laughter never fade,
An old-fashioned Christmas, serenely made.

So may you find peace in this quiet cheer,
And treasure the magic of yesteryear.
A gift of joy, both calm and bright,
Held in your heart this Christmas night.